Emotional Intelligence

*How To Understand Emotions
And Raise Your EQ*

Josephine T. Lewis

Contents

CHAPTER 1: THE DIFFERENCE BETWEEN EQ AND IQ

It is commonly believed that a person's IQ score determines how smart they are or how successful they will be. However, this score is far from the entire picture as far as someone's overall intelligence goes.

What is IQ and What does it say about You?

Your IQ is meant to measure your ability to learn new information, exercise memory, see patterns, and use logic. A good test for IQ will measure how well you are at processing visual-spatial information, auditory input, your short-term memory, and how fast you are at general mental processing. Your IQ is supposed to say how well you will handle learning new information and applying it to your life.

What is EQ and What does it say about You?

Your EQ is how well you can understand the feelings of yourself and others, what motivates people, and how to

1

effectively work along with them. For many individuals, their EQ (or level of emotional intelligence) is much more important than their IQ as far as how successful they will be in their careers and general life. Today, our personal and professional success rely heavily on how well we can read signals, both in ourselves and others, and respect them in the appropriate ways.

Although IQ does matter as far as how smart a person is, without the social and emotional skills to manage their intelligence, a person will not get far in life. Without the ability to understand the importance of cooperation, existing within the world is a struggle. This means that everyone should work on developing and maturing their skills of emotional intelligence, since they are needed to empathize with, understand, and negotiate with others. This is especially relevant since our world is becoming more and more connected as society progresses. There are a few key qualities that emotional intelligence comprises of, and each is equally important.

The Key Categories of a Person's Emotional Intelligence:

- **Awareness of Self:** This refers to being able to recognize feelings as they happen. To develop this skill, you must be able to tune into and identify what you are truly feeling. Once you are able to evaluate the feelings going on inside of you, you can effectively work with them and manage them. Someone who is self-aware knows themselves, their own mind, and their heart. They pay attention to inner signals and heed them.

The main factors of true self-awareness are the ability to recognize feelings (be aware of your emotions and notice how they affect your life) and confidence of self (certainty about your capabilities and self-worth).

- **Regulation of Self:** Most people do not have much control over when they will experience feelings. They can, however, learn to have a say in the length of time that feeling will last by consciously learning methods for alleviating negative feelings like depression, anxiety, or anger. Some of those methods deal with reframing a situation mentally to seem more positive, engaging in prayer, taking walks, or practicing meditation.

Self-regulation includes the ability to control yourself and manage impulses that could be disruptive. It also deals with how trustworthy and honest you are (personal integrity). It has to do with being able to take responsibility for the way you act, how well you adapt to new situations, and how open

3

you are to new thoughts and ideas (those of yourself and others).

- **Personal Motivation:** The ability to motivate yourself for your goals requires a clear cut vision of what your goals are and an attitude of optimism. People do generally have a predisposition to thinking more positively or more negatively, but thinking optimistically can occur with practice and plenty of effort. When you learn how to catch a pessimistic thought or feeling as it happens, you can take steps to reframe it more positively, meaning that you can accomplish your goals easier.

  Motivation is made up of your drive to achieve (how much you want to improve and reach an excellent standard) and your level of commitment (on a personal or group level). It also consists of your initiative (how well you respond to and act on chances and opportunities in life) and optimism (persisting in your goals despite setbacks and obstacles).

- **A Strong Empathetic Sense:** Empathy is about knowing how to recognize the way people feel. This ability is important for success both in personal relationships and your professional life. The better

4

you are at discerning the emotions that lie behind the signals of others, the easier you can control which signals you are sending to others.

Empathetic people are highly skilled at service work, which entails meeting and recognizing the needs of clients and customers. They are also good at helping others grow and develop (sensing the direction in which people need to grow and aiding them in this pursuit). They are good at using diversity to their advantage and cultivating unique opportunities with people of all walks of life. Empathetic types excel in reading the emotional torrents of groups, as well as relationships of power between individuals and understanding the wants and needs of other people.

- **Skills in Socializing:** Developing quality skills on an interpersonal level is imperative to your success with your career and life in general. In our modern world of constant connection, nearly every person has access to data at their fingertips. This means that people skills are becoming more crucial. You have to have a high level of emotional intelligence to better empathize with, understand, and negotiate among people in a united social structure and economy.

With high social skills comes the power of influence (being effectively persuasive with others), being communicative (being able to send messages clearly to others), and effective leadership (the ability to inspire and guide others). People with great social skills also know how to be the catalyst for change and manage it and manage conflict by resolving issues and negotiating. They can also build meaningful bonds, cooperate and collaborate toward a shared vision or goal, and manage team abilities.

These valuable characteristics in both personal life and business show that people with high IQs are not always the best equipped to succeed. Someone with a more modest number on their IQ can still win if they have high emotional intelligence. How well you will perform has to do with both types of intelligence. In fact, experts say that IQ only accounts for up to 10 percent of your likelihood of succeeding. Reading all of this would, understandably, make you want to understand more about the ins and outs of emotional intelligence. What does this unique kind of intelligence entail and how can you get more of it? This book will cover all of that, and more, in the following chapters.

CHAPTER 2: THE DOWNSIDES OF A LOW EQ

If having a high level of emotional intelligence helps people succeed, it only stands to reason that lacking this quality would have plenty of downsides. If you neglect to pay attention to or develop this in yourself, what do you stand to lose? Let's look at some of the specific consequences that happen as a result of a low level of emotional intelligence.

What are the Consequences of Having Low Emotional Intelligence?

- **Motivation Problems:** Everyone has great ideas, but only a few go on to succeed from those ideas. Why is that? It's because some people know how to motivate themselves into action once they have the idea, while others simply have the idea and don't do anything about it. Having a high level of emotional intelligence means that you know exactly how to motivate yourself into action.

You can call upon feelings, at will, and get yourself
to get moving and make things happen. Again, this
has little to do with having an exceptionally high IQ.
A high IQ won't get you far if you can't get yourself
to take action toward your goals.

- **Struggling with Feelings:** Feelings are not always
easy to bear, but it becomes easier once you start
developing your EQ. Someone without the emotional
intelligence to recognize what it is they are feeling
are a lot more likely to become frozen by
overwhelming emotions. This could be a feeling of
insecurity, anger, or simple anxiety.

  With a high EQ, you can recognize when you are
feeling something, such as fear, and look beyond it to
see real solutions. Emotional intelligence at its core
is about knowing that feelings pass and don't have to
control your life if you don't let them. However, not
understanding this will make it hard to decipher
what is real and what is simply a strong emotion.

- **Becoming Easily Overwhelmed:** When someone
doesn't have the self-awareness to recognize what
they are feeling, it has a tendency to get very
overwhelming. They don't understand why this
strong emotion seems to be taking them over and

filling their mind. However, with emotional intelligence, you can recognize what is happening and find a way to deal with it. This could be anything from taking a break when you need it to having a talk with a friend when it's necessary.

Overwhelm can be prevented by recognizing the signs that lead up to such a state. When a strong feeling appears, a self-aware and emotionally intelligent person can look at it and refer back to past situations where this feeling appeared, then choose to make a conscious and mature decision for dealing with it.

- **Trouble Relating to Others:** People who lack emotional intelligence have a hard time reading their own emotions, which makes it nearly impossible to truly relate to others. Not only does the preoccupation with what's going on in their own heads take over, but they wouldn't have the easiest time reading the emotions of others even if they were paying attention. When someone has a low EQ, they may often find themselves at odds with people they truly care about and wondering what has happened.

No matter how much they try to relate their side of the story, they find themselves misunderstood. This is because reading the emotions of others does not come easily to them. Luckily, this is a skill that can be developed with effort, and even people who have had terrible luck in this department previously can improve greatly.

Considering the above information, knowing whether you need to work on your EQ is highly important. So, how do you know if you have low emotional intelligence?

Here are Some Signs that you Need to Work on your EQ:

- **Your Work Performance is Suffering Regularly:** Research has proven that most of the highest performers in career places have a high level of emotional intelligence and that the lowest performers do not. It's not impossible that someone with a low EQ will perform well at work, but they don't have as good of a chance. A high EQ at work means you know how to manage emotions that could stand in the way of success.

  You may notice that you consistently have arguments with customers, or that you can't seem to get along with anyone at the office. You may find yourself in constant conflict with others without being sure of why. This could be the answer you've been looking for.

- **You are Highly Critical of Other People:** Are you a person who likes to gossip about others and talk down about them to your co-workers? This type of insecure behavior typically shows that someone does not have a very high level of emotional intelligence. People with high emotional intelligence tend to look for solutions when they have an issue with others. Having a high EQ means having a high level of empathy for others.

- **You Lose your Temper Often:** Some people think that having an angry reaction to something in your life is a bad thing, but that simply isn't true. Experiencing anger or irritation is just a part of being human, and none of us are robots and shouldn't try to act like one. However, if any criticism you receive from a friend, your spouse, or even someone you don't know well gets under your skin, it could be a sign of a deeper issue.

Maybe you find yourself getting mad when watching certain programs on television or when overhearing a conversation next to you on the bus. If any minor criticism you receive from a person in your life leads to a blowup, there is definitely a sign here that you should work on your emotional intelligence.

- **When you have Trouble Working with Others:** When a person doesn't have a high level of emotional intelligence, they have a difficult time relating to the needs, ideas, and suggestions of other people, even in group project situations at work. Being part of a group means that you know how to listen to others and use their feedback to improve your performance. If you have a hard time paying attention to the suggestions of others, for whatever reason, it's a sign that your EQ needs work.

  This also applies in leadership positions. If you find yourself overcome with the need to lead others or be the position of authority and you focus more on competition than team efforts, you should probably try to improve your emotional intelligence. Leaders who never stop to think about what the people working for them think and regularly show angry outbursts or take advantage of their power positions will likely not be effective leaders.

- **Problems at Work or Home are Never your Fault:** Think back to the last few conflicts you've had either with personal relations or people at work. Who was at fault in those situations? If you answer that it was other people every time, this could be a sign that you need to work on your emotional intelligence. It's true that sometimes we work with difficult people that are hard to get along with or have that specific family member that always gets under our skin; but if you cannot think of one time recently that you were at fault, this shows that you are not being very realistic.

- **You don't Care about Whether you Get Along with Co-Workers:** It isn't necessary to need everyone you meet to like you, but if you find that you consistently don't get along with people at work and don't care about it, you may have a low emotional intelligence. Having a peaceful work environment matters, and getting along with colleagues is part of i.

Perhaps you have noticed that some of the above points fit you. If you recognized yourself in any of the paragraphs above, you need to start working on raising your EQ level. Luckily, this can be done through effort and practice, and there are some specific strategies you can start implementing to improve your emotional intelligence today.

<u>Tips for becoming More Emotionally Intelligent</u>:

- **Listen to Feedback from Others:** It's impossible to improve a personal problem that you don't fully understand yourself. One of the most important elements of having emotional intelligence is being aware of yourself, meaning that you recognize and stay conscious of your own behavior in the present. Whether this entails listening to a full on assessment of yourself or just asking a select few trusted people for their honest feedback, this is a critical step for improving your personal sense of how you are acting or not acting.

  The key here is to refrain from making excuses for the things you do or do not do. This will defeat the entire purpose of the exercise. Instead, you need to listen to the criticisms others are giving you, attempt to fully understand what they are saying, and own up to all of it. Some people initially feel offensive when they receive feedback, but if you can take a moment to think and process it, you can own it, move forward, and find ways to change.

- **Be Aware of the Difference between Intention and Result:** People who don't have a strong sense of emotional intelligence have a tendency to underestimate the negative influence what they say and do can have on those around them. They don't pay attention to the space between the words they speak and the way that others accept these words.

In spite of what the intentions behind your words are, give some thought to the way your words are going to affect and influence other people, and whether this is the reaction you want them to have to what you are saying to them. Some people have a reputation for saying certain things that others didn't take so kindly to, but they can begin to think about their words and the impact they actually have on other people.

If this applies to you, you're probably wondering what can be done to fix it. So, how can you improve this in yourself? To work on this, you can begin asking yourself what impression you wish to have on others. You can also ask what you wish others would think about you once you have spoken, and how you can specifically reframe your words to make that happen in reality.

- **Learn how to Pause when Necessary:** Having a high level of EQ means knowing how to make intentional decisions about how you will react and respond to stimuli, instead of succumbing to your first knee-jerk impulse. You might, for example, have a tendency to shoot down or interrupt the ideas of others before they even have a chance to finish their sentence. Acting this way shows that you are reacting to a fear inside, that you may lose control of the talk or even waste precious and valuable time.

A great way to combat this impulse is to learn how to pause when necessary before you respond. You can do this in a couple of different ways. First, you can learn to pause in order to listen to your own inner thoughts. When you find yourself getting frustrated and impatient in talking with others, you might notice that you have a tendency to clench your fists. Learn to recognize these signs of stress and use them to trigger you to notice that you might be losing control of yourself.

This can lead to you being able to choose how you will react instead of defaulting to your typical responses that might be destructive. Take some time to take a breath, pause, and try listening to the people around you. To truly listen means that you are aiding others in feeling understood, regardless of whether you agree with what they are saying or not. This is not comparable to not speaking. This means allowing others an opportunity to give their input and opinions before you have to voice your own.

- **Wear another Person's Shoes, while Wearing yours:** This can also be described as wearing both shoes. A lot of people say that you should walk a mile in another person's shoes in order to understand where they are coming from and develop empathy. This is an important aspect of having emotional intelligence. However, you should never put aside your feelings in favor of this.

  Instead, you should put on both shoes, meaning that you are aware of your own agenda along with the other person's and are viewing everything from both points of view. You can learn to change your approach from focusing only on your concerns to sharing your own thoughts and then openly listening to the other person's concerns. This can lead you to find out ways that will please both parties.

If you recognized yourself in the areas above, don't worry. If your emotional intelligence is low, you can consciously improve it, and being aware of what needs works is the only way to make changes. Raising your EQ will take discipline, commitment, and your belief in the importance of it. If you dedicate yourself to this task and give it some time, however, you will see that the effort you made to get there was well worth it.

CHAPTER 3: HOW CAN EMOTIONAL INTELLIGENCE BENEFIT YOU?

The concept of emotional intelligence is rising in popularity with research in psychology in more recent times, especially since it has a direct effect on today's workforce. Companies are made up of people, so whatever impacts the successfulness and productivity of people will also have a direct impact on the company they are working for or running. Actually, experts in psychology believe now that the level a person's EQ at is a better indicator than most other things of how successful and happy that person will be in life.

The Evolution of this Concept, and What it Means:

It's quite fascinating to look at the way the concept of EQ has changed and evolved throughout the years. Back in 1930, this concept started out simply as "social intelligence" and grew into a term known as "emotional strength" a couple of decades later. In modern day, the terms have been blended and are now known as emotional intelligence.

Whatever you wish to call it, however, emotional intelligence means recognizing and understanding your own reactions and emotions and managing them to adapt and control feelings, moods, responses, and reactions. This leads to the ability to motivate yourself to follow through with, commit to, and work on goals. What good is a high level of intelligence if you can't motivate yourself to use it?

How Emotional Intelligence helps us Relate to Others:

But emotional intelligence is about more than this. It also deals with discerning the emotions of other people, having an understanding of what they feel, and using that awareness to better relate to other people. This is absolutely crucial for building relationships, relating to people in social scenarios, leading others, working through issues and conflict, and being part of a group structure (or having social skills). In addition to these points, there are some other reasons why EQ is crucial in life.

How does having a High EQ Benefit your Life?

More Inner-peace: When you have a high level of emotional intelligence, you feel more at ease with yourself because you are able to achieve your goals and stick to your plan, no matter what comes up. Since only your emotional reactions can truly disturb you, and you already know how to deal with yours, you can go through life in a poised manner and handle everything with calm self-assuredness.

You can encounter stressful situations at work, difficult co-workers, and traffic jams, all with a sense of inner peace. Having a high EQ means you are well mentally. How much intelligence you have emotionally has a direct effect on your outlook and attitude in life. It will help you with alleviating anxious feelings and staying away from severe mood swings and depression. A high EQ is related to happier outlooks and optimistic viewpoints.

Better Health on a Physical Level: Knowing how to care for yourself and to manage your own levels of stress is related to your emotional intelligence. When you are mentally healthy, you have more energy and are more likely to make healthy choices about fitness and activity. You will also have less of a tendency to crave junk food and other unhealthy physical activities. Only once you are aware of the state of your reactions and emotions, you can start managing your stress levels and working toward better overall health.

Better Relationships: When you can better understand and therefore manage, your feelings, you can start to share them with others in a way that comes across effectively and is constructive. You will also be able to better understand the people you are in relationships with. You are less likely to misinterpret what your loved one says, and you are better able to understand how they feel and empathize with it. Being aware of the feelings, responses, and needs of the ones we care for will lead us to relationships that are more fulfilling and stronger all around.

The Ability to Resolve Conflict: When you are able to discern the feelings of others and truly see their point of view, you will find it a lot simpler to fix conflicts or just avoid them altogether before they can happen. You will also become better at coming to agreements when issues arise since you will be more aware of the needs of other people. After all, how can you give someone what they need if you aren't aware of what they need?

In addition to this, you will be better with conflict resolution when you have a high EQ because you will be more approachable to other people. They will know that they can expect from you and be truly heard and empathized with, making it easier for them to trust you.

Leadership Skills: A high EQ often correlates with strong leadership skills. In other words, it goes along with knowing what motivates people, how to relate to them in a positive way, and foster and develop greater bonds with those around you. This means that people who have a higher level of emotional intelligence are much better at leading people.

A great leader recognizes what people around them need, and makes sure that those needs are met using methods that engender satisfaction and high performance at work. A leader who is intelligent and savvy with their feelings and those of others is also to build up strong teams. This is done by recognizing and utilizing the diversity of team members on an emotional level in a way that will benefit the entire team, as well as the business.

Self-honesty and Growth: High emotional intelligence means that you are always growing and looking for ways to improve yourself. This comes along with the ability to be honest with yourself about your shortcomings so that you can work to change them. A person with a high EQ does not shy away from truths, even when they aren't the most pleasant things to realize.

While other people who are less emotionally intelligent would shy away from this type of introspection, the emotionally mature person just takes it as part of life's course, and for this reason is always growing. They do not miss out on chances to improve because they don't want to accept criticism.

The Ability to Achieve Goals and Succeed in Life: A higher EQ lets you motivate yourself when you need it, meaning that you are not a procrastinator, have high levels of confidence, and know how to get yourself to focus when necessary. This quality will also let you create better relationships with others, improving your support system when things go awry in life.

With a high level of emotional intelligence, you will be better able to overcome unforeseen circumstances and complications and stick to your goals with an adaptable perspective and positive outlook. Small setbacks will not throw you off or make you doubt your plan, and you don't waste any time getting hung up on things you can't change. Knowing how to delay satisfaction and keep a long term vision in mind will directly impact whether or not you succeed in life.

Emotional intelligence is a subject that is still being studied and is not entirely understood yet. However, we are aware of the fact that it is highly important, even more so than our level of general intelligence in the brain. Our feelings, and how we choose to manage and live with them, play a large role in how our lives will go both on a professional and personal level. Improving this part of ourselves means that we will raise the quality of our lives. Although technology and tools go a long way to help humans master and learn information, there is nothing that can take the place of our ability to effectively deal with our feelings and the feelings of people in our lives.

Emotional Intelligence is Something we all Recognize:

It is the boss at a restaurant who remains calm and respectful to the customer yelling obnoxiously about the service or the reasonable friend you rely on when you need someone levelheaded to talk to. The rescue workers who stays poised and compassionate as they help people suffering from a natural disaster, or the significant other who rarely gets angry, will easily forgive you, and takes responsibility for their own feelings and actions.

How about that successful head of the company who manages to keep her job, family obligations, and extracurricular activities with confidence and peacefulness? What is it about all of these people that makes them so skilled with life? To put it simply, it's their emotional intelligence, of course.

A Somewhat New, but Important Definition:

This concept is new compared to other psychological terms, but EQ has been around since humans have. It's the ability to manage emotions instead of allowing them to spin out of control and become destructive. It's also the ability to make other people happy and calm or help them handle situations better. People with a high level of this particular kind of intelligence have been shown to become more prosperous in their lives. Whether it be a professional or social environment, these personality types strive and thrive, succeeding in all areas.

What do Emotionally Intelligent People Stay Away from?

Plenty of research has shown that people with a high EQ have fewer issues mentally, including anxiety and depression. They have healthy personal lives, instead of train wreck relationships, because they live from meaningful and thoughtful decisions. They perform at the highest level at work, excelling in the workplace and being engaged in happy relationships. They also regularly work for getting great results in all areas of their lives. What kind of activities does this type of person avoid?

Getting Caught in Drama: We've already gone over the fact that empathy goes hand in hand with emotional intelligence, and people with a high EQ will show this quality to all people in their lives. However, there's a distinct difference between showing empathy for loved ones and friends and letting someone else's misery or rage take over or influence your own life. We all know someone who gets upset at the smallest flip of a switch, allowing other people to get to them.

Or someone who is drawn to drama in a pattern-seeking way and uses it to distract themselves from their own issues.

Someone with a high level of emotional intelligence will not get caught up in other people's drama, but will instead listen thoughtfully and give careful and loving advice. They will also help however they can without letting someone else's reactions and drama influence their life to a negative degree.

Complaining: Grumbling and whining about life shows a couple of different things. One, that no solutions are possible to our issues and two, that we are constantly feeling victimized by life. Someone with a high EQ will rarely feel like the victim, and even rare than this will they feel as though a solution to an issue is out of their reach or impossible. Rather than searching for a person or situation to blame for where they are, they are already searching for solutions on fixing the problem.

In other words, they are too busy finding answers to problems to complain about them. They are also aware of the fact that complaining will have an impact on the feelings of people they are talking to, and they don't wish to do that. So, instead of complaining or gossiping to friends when something goes wrong, in essence, sharing their misery, they search for constructive ways to feel better. This can mean opening up to a person and seeking advice, journaling about the issue, or going on a solitary walk.

They Know how to Say No: Similar to empathy, conviction and the ability to control oneself are hallmarks of a person who is emotionally healthy. People with a high EQ know that having more wine at the dinner party will lead them to feel worse when they wake up, or that saying yes to the spontaneous invitation that evening will make them less likely to follow through on commitments that were already made.

They make the choice to be definitive when it comes to making choices instead of defaulting to uncertain answers, maybes, or "I don't knows". They are aware that uncertain language, such as "Maybe I don't really need to work out today", is inviting doubt into their minds, which leads to a higher level of anxiety and possibly, in extreme cases, depression and regret. Doubtful language has no place in their minds.

A person with a high EQ knows that the more often they say no to unnecessary or negative situations, and the more they exercise their own self-control and willpower and the better off they will be in focusing their way to achieving goals and overall happiness in life.

They are not Gossipers: Someone with a solid emotional intelligence will avoid gossip just as certainly as they will avoid drama. They don't feel the need to engage in the scandalous chats of their co-workers or shame other people for mistakes they might have made. This is because they are secure in themselves and gossip is usually an indicator of insecurity. They are not tempted to join in on talks where another person is being brought down.

It's also because they don't feel like they have a right to judge what constitutes a mistake for another person, since mistakes can often just be a chance to improve and grow. The fact that they are not gossipers makes them easier to trust for other people, which contributes to healthier, deeper friendships and relationships.

They never Rely on Other People for Confidence or Happiness: Having a healthy, strong EQ means being self-sufficient when it comes to life, including your own peace of mind and contentment. When you feel down, you realize that it's your feeling to deal with and you seek out proactive ways to do this. People who are emotionally intelligent and mature already know that counting on others for their sense of worthiness or happiness can only lead to hopelessness and disappointment.

Instead of doing this, they take responsibility for their own feelings, searching for hobbies that are enjoyable to them, striving to accomplish goals that will deepen their self-love, and finding acceptance instead of themselves. Both praise and slander have little to no effect on a person with a high

EQ, because their sense of worth does not come from others.

They Stay Away from Talking Badly about Themselves: In addition to not gossiping about others, an emotionally solid person does not gossip about or slander themselves. It is true that nearly everyone has thought or said negative things about themselves like "I am a failure" or "I am ugly". However, emotionally intelligent people know how to cut off those thoughts right as they come up instead of getting caught up in them.

Rather than getting lost in irrational thought loops about self-negativity, they look to facts to base their conclusions on. To some people, this could be looking at their achievements and experience on a resume, or the orderliness of their house or car, or a simple inventory check on everything that is going right in their lives at that moment.

What it comes down to is being able to recognize that negative feelings and thoughts are just thoughts and don't have to control things or run your life. Getting caught up in a cycle of negativity just because a worry crossed your mind is ludicrous, and people with a high emotional intelligence know that. For this reason, when they hear that negative voice inside, they know to stop listening or turn it down, staying focused on their day and goals.

They Rarely Waste their Time on Regret: When someone exists mostly in the past, instead of in the present moment, they are leaving themselves open to a whole load of spiritual and mental issues, from agitation to nostalgia to intense regret. People with emotional intelligence respect their past, including their own mistakes and the people they have known or loved from the past. However, they know how to do this while also honoring their life in the present moment.

They are aware that becoming too focused on aspects of life that cannot be changed is wasting opportunities in the moment and only taking away from their focus. By committing to learning from mistakes (rather than getting caught up on regretting them), they have the control over what will happen in the present and approach it with gratitude, hope, and self-love.

If you have noticed any of the above activities in yourself, it can be a sign that you have some work to do on your emotional intelligence. If you have decided that you want to commit to fixing this in yourself, there are some activities you can start working on right now, which we are going to take a look at in the following chapter.

CHAPTER 4: WHICH ACTIVITIES RAISE YOUR EQ?

As we've stated earlier in the book, your EQ or emotional intelligence refers to your ability to be aware of, manage, and express your emotions in addition to doing this with people around you. Most people who perform well in areas that require talent or dedication have a high emotional intelligence, while low performers do not. This particular brand of intelligence is very important for forming, developing, enhancing, and maintaining meaningful, close relationships with other people. While IQ cannot be significantly changed throughout life, your EQ can increase, grow, and develop along with your desire to improve and grow.

How can you begin Improving your Emotional Intelligence?

Work on Reducing Negative Feelings: This might be the most important factor of all when it comes to EQ: managing your own bad feelings and not letting them take over you and become destructive. For this to happen and to effectively change your feelings toward a situation, you have to change how you think of it first. How can you start to change how you think of situations in a negative light?

1. **Stop Personalizing the Behavior of Others:** One way to start to reframe situations in your life more positively is to stop personalizing situations that happen. Next time you feel negatively about the way a person is behaving, try to stop yourself from jumping to a bad conclusion immediately. Rather, think of a few different ways you can look at the situation instead of having a knee-jerk reaction.

   Perhaps you saw a friend at a party and they didn't greet you. This may lead you to start wondering if they don't like you anymore, or you can come up with alternatives such as the fact that they didn't see you or were exceptionally busy at that moment. When you learn to stop taking the behavior of others so personally, you can be more objective about what they express. People act because of themselves and not due to us. Broadening your perspective will lessen the chances of misunderstanding others.

2. **Getting rid of your Rejection Fear:** A great way to address and handle your fear of being rejected is to give yourself more than one option in situations that

are important. This way, regardless of what ends up happening, you already have a list of alternatives to move on with. Avoid placing all importance on just one situation and focusing solely on your fear of rejection, such as thinking "If I don't get this job, my life is over".

Instead, focus on solutions and alternatives, such as telling yourself that if that job doesn't work out, there are a couple of others you can try out. Already have a list with the jobs written down so you have a physical reminder of this, and that way, if things don't go as you hope, you won't be as devastated.

Work on your Ability to Remain Calm: A lot of us feel stressed out in at least one area of life. The way you handle situations that are stressful is what decides whether you are assertive or simply being reactive or calm versus falling apart. Next time you are in a stressful situation, you should try to remember to stay calm and collected. Follow these tips next time:

1. **Take a Pause:** Next time you are feeling anxious or nervous, splash your face with water and take a walk to get some air. Lowering body heat can help reduce levels of anxiety. You should also avoid caffeine which can worsen the issue.

2. **Engage in Intense Activity:** If you're finding yourself depressed, fearful, or discouraged, you can try out some intense workout exercises and get energized instead. How you move your body in life will directly impact how you are feeling, and motion directly influences what emotion you will feel. You will also increase your confidence this way when you feel what your body can do.

Learn how to Express Feelings and be Assertive: In order to be emotionally healthy and well-rounded, you have to be able to openly talk about what matters to you, even when it's difficult. This involves taking a clear stand on issues, clarifying what is or is not acceptable to you, and more. We all have situations in life that call for the setting of boundaries in order to make it clear what we will or will not tolerate. This can mean disagreeing respectfully, knowing how to say no, be free of guilt, or seek self-protection. Here is how to work on this:

- **Use XYZ Communication:** Next time you have an emotion that you need to express and are finding it difficult, use this technique. You state how you feel (X), when a specific thing happens (Y) in a particular situation (Z). For example, "I feel irritated that you are asking me to put aside my plans to help you."

- **Avoid Accusatory Language:** Try to stay away from using statements that start with the word "you" and are followed by a judgment or accusation. This type of language will automatically make the person listening feel defensive, even if that is not your intention, and a lot less open to what you are saying.

Learn how to be Proactive with Difficult People: This is a hard one, because difficult people often make us want to react. The majority of us will experience people who are hard to deal with in day to day life. This may end up with you getting stuck with someone at home or work, which can make it easy to let your day be ruined. However, how are some better ways for handling a challenging situation?

1. **Try Counting:** This is common advice, but it's for a good reason; it works. Next time you are getting upset or angry at someone, rather than opening your mouth to speak immediately, try to breathe deeply and count to 10. With most situations, once you reach 10, a better solution will have made itself clear to you. Having taken the time to figure out a positive alternative to reacting in anger, you will help to solve or reduce the issue instead of making it more complicated. If it turns out you're still upset after counting, talk a walk if you can and return once you are calm.

2. **Put Yourself in their Position:** Another method you can use to lessen reactivity is to place yourself in another person's position for a few seconds. One way to do this is to think about the person in question and imagine what it is about their situation that is difficult.

   This does not clear up or excuse intolerable actions or behavior. This exercise simply exists as a way to remind you that the way people act is a result of what they are encountering in their own personal lives, and it isn't always easy. If you manage to stay considerate and reasonable, the way someone else acts is reveals more about them than us. When you learn to de-personalize, you can see the scenario in a more objective light, leading to healthy, productive solutions.

3. **Make Consequences Clear:** Knowing how to come up with and state consequences is an important way to assert your position when it comes to encountering someone difficult. If you can effectively state this a consequence will allow the difficult person to pause and change from a position of violation to one of basic respect.

Work on Recovering from Hard Situations: Michael Jordan has stated that he has missed thousands and thousands of shots during his sports career, and hundreds of games. He has failed so many times but keeps going, which is why he is successful. Life can be quite difficult and everyone is aware of it. The way we decide to think, act, and feel in response to the challenges of life will decide whether you are in hope or despair, happiness versus depression, or winning versus losing.

Along with every situation that is hard or challenging, you can ask yourself where the lesson is, in what ways you can learn from it, or what solutions might exist out there. The better we get at asking these questions, the better our answers will be. Learn how to ask yourself questions that are constructive and based upon priorities and learning and this will let you gain the right perspective and handle any situation that comes up.

What Other Steps can be Taken to Improve your EQ?

- **Learn how to Share Intimate Feelings in Relationships:** Knowing how to validate and express loving, tender feelings effectively is a must for having and developing close relationships with others. What this means is knowing how to share these thoughts in a way that is constructive and nourishing and knowing how to respond positively when someone extends such feelings to you.

- **Start Observing your Feelings:** As we go about our busy lives, rushing from place to place and taking on projects, it's easy to lose track of our feelings. But when you do that, you are a lot less likely to act consciously or carefully. You may also miss out on important signals or information within our emotions. Next time you notice that you are having a strong reaction to what is happening, try to remember that you are getting important information about an event, person, or situation.

Your reaction could be because of what is happening now, or you might be getting reminded of a memory that has been unprocessed and is painful. When you make it a point to notice how you feel, you will start trusting your feelings more often, allowing you to become better at controlling and managing them. In order to get better at it, you can try this.

Set some alarms to go off throughout your day. Each time the alarm sounds, breathe deeply and pay attention to what your feelings are at that time. Notice where the feeling is manifesting as a physical sensation, and what that sensation is like. After doing this for a while, you will get used to it and do it automatically.

- **Start Noticing your Behavior:** As we have stated throughout this book, improving your emotional intelligence is all about knowing how to manage your own feelings, which is only possible when you know what they are. As you get better at becoming aware of your emotions, make sure you are paying attention to how you behave, as well. Pay attention to the way you behave when certain feelings come up and what effect this has on your life. Do these feelings influence the way you speak to others, how productive you are, or how good you feel throughout the day?

  As soon as you start to notice the way you react to your feelings, it can be easy to start judging yourself or labeling your reactions and behavior. It's important that you avoid doing this, since you will find it easier to be honest if you aren't receiving self-judgment simultaneously.

- **Start being Accountable for How you Act and Feel:** Out of this list, this one that is most difficult, but it is also very helpful. The feelings you experience and the way you behave is all the result of you yourself, not other people, meaning that it is you and you alone who is responsible. If your feelings are hurt as a reaction to what someone else said and it causes you to lash out, you are accountable for that reaction. That person did not make you react the way you did, and your reaction is up to you, always.

In the same way, your emotions can allow you access to important information pertaining to how you experience what someone else does along with your preferences and needs; but that doesn't make your emotions the responsibility of another person. As soon as you commit to being accountable for the way you feel and act, it will benefit your life in many ways.

- **Know the Difference between a Response and a Reaction:** A key to becoming emotionally intelligent is the practice of learning to respond instead of react. At first glance, these may seem like synonymous terms, but there is a subtle and important distinction between the two. A reaction is a process that is unconscious and comes about from being triggered emotionally, then behaving in a way that relieves our feeling. An example of this would be lashing out at someone who interrupts you while talking.

Responding, on the other hand, is an activity that

relies on staying conscious and aware. It has to do with paying attention to what you are feeling and then making a choice for how to behave. Sticking with the example above, it would mean that when someone interrupts you, you explain how it made you feel, why you don't like it, and request that they refrain from that in the future, all while staying respectful with your tone.

- **Making Empathy a Regular Practice:** This involves both yourself and other people in your life and will raise your EQ level. Empathy means having an understanding of the way a person behaves and feels, as well as making an effort to communicate with and understand them. You can begin this by yourself. Next time you notice that you are feeling something or behaving a specific way, ask yourself why it is happening.

You may find that your first reaction is to answer that you don't know; but if you continue to stay aware of your emotions and the way you behave, various answers will begin to make themselves clear to you. This will pave the way to more conscious behavior and responses rather than possibly harmful reactions.

- **Become more Positive:** In addition to the practices we already mentioned (including empathy, being responsible for yourself, and awareness), set aside some time to pay attention to the areas of life that are going great and what you are thankful for. This type of attitude is contagious to others and will foster an environment of positivity, improving your overall life quality.

- **Keeping a Progress Journal:** A great way to stay motivated and inspired on your journey to emotional intelligence is to keep a progress journal. You can write down the specific steps that you want to start working on and then each day you can record how successful you were, what went right, what could use some more work, and how you can improve.

  It's not always easy to see the ways in which we are progressing throughout life, so keeping a record that allows you to go back and see how far you've come can be extremely helpful for staying motivated and engaged. This will also help you come up with your own creative solutions for improving your EQ.

- **Meeting a lot of New People:** One of the best ways to develop empathy is to surround yourself with different people often, particularly when those people already have the traits that you wish to acquire. When we spend time around people who are reflective, empathetic, and non-reactive, it starts rubbing off on us after a while.

On the other hand, encountering people who are difficult can give us valuable practice in staying non-reactive when we get upset. If you simply look for them, opportunities to learn and improve are all around you every day.

Keep in Mind, this is Lifelong Work:

Emotional intelligence is not a pursuit that you can achieve overnight and then just forget about. This practice will be with you for life, and there are always areas to improve, no matter how far you get. Even if you have done great at the steps listed above, don't slack off and always continue practicing. This will allow you to benefit from this practice forever.

Chapter 5: Emotional Intelligence and Relationships

Do you wish that your relationship was better or closer? If so, you don't need to visit a therapist for couples. Instead, you can improve your relations by applying emotional intelligence to the mix. We've gone over what the term means: using your feelings and moods to effectively live your life and have a positive impact. In order to work on developing this and applying it to your life, you can follow through with the exercises listed in the last chapter. These will help you manage your emotions and gain the skills needed to help you interact with other people in a better way.

How can EQ Improve your Relationship?

No matter what problem you are facing in your relationship, you can improve it. As we've already mentioned in previous chapters, people with high emotional intelligence enjoy success in more areas than people who don't, and close relationships are no exception to this. Think about it this way: does anyone ever think about leaving their marriage because they have a partner who is too attentive, too understanding, or too encouraging and supportive? Once you apply EQ to the relationship you have with your partner, you can miraculously transform it. But where should you begin?

Building up Awareness in your Relationship:

A high awareness of self will let you know what emotional factors you need in order to thrive and be happy. For a relationship to thrive and be happy, however, you and your significant other need to become aware of which emotional factors are needed so you can help each other meet your needs. The reason why people get into relationships in the first place is because these factors were being met when the relationship began.

Necessary Emotional Factors and How to Find them:

But the factors we need to thrive and grow are always changing, meaning that having EQ here refers to staying aware of those factors and whether they are being met on both sides. As soon as partners can sense that their relationship is helping them to grow in to a better person, they will want to continue it. Here are the steps to doing this:

- Make a List of the Emotional Factors you Need: Here you will write down the top three emotional factors needed for you to feel fulfilled in a relationship. Have your partner do the same.

- Make a List of the Factors you think They Need: Now you will write down what you believe are the top three emotional factors needed by your partner in order to feel fulfilled. Have them also make a list for you.

- Trade Lists: Now you will trade lists and each read them and have a discussion afterwards. This will allow you to come up with new ideas for meeting the necessary emotional factors for each of you.

Identifying and Managing Emotions in your Relationship:

Important results from research on emotions has proven that they play a direct role in how well (or poorly) people perform. Certain feelings like anxiety or anger can nourish or stand in the way of relationships, while feelings such as optimism, enthusiasm, and confidence have a tendency to make them more productive. One emotion that nearly always gets in the way and has long term negative effects is depression. What this implies is that relationships able to handle anxiety or anger in a positive way and that stay away from depression and nurture optimism, enthusiasm, and confidence will become healthier and more rewarding.

Why you should Know about Contagious Emotions:

Why is it so hard to manage your feelings in a relationship? It's the landscape that happens as a result of you and your partner's feelings that involves the contagion of emotions. This refers to the fact that feelings are similar to a virus in how they can spread between people. You can actually catch the anxiety, depression, or anger of your partner, or you can infect your loved one with your own enthusiasm and confidence.

How to Use this Phenomenon to your Advantage:

In order to use this phenomenon to benefit your relationship, you have to know how to manage the feelings that are influencing your relations. Here are some skills you can work on for this.

- **Learn how to Relax at Will:** If you can make yourself relax at will, it shows that you know how to regulate your feelings. This will let you become immunized against negative emotions from your partner, letting you keep perspective, which has a tendency to get lost when both partners are in a bad state of mind. Negative feelings like depression or anxiety will heighten your feeling arousal and lead to a rigidity in your mental state, making it harder to act productively and accurately interpret what is happening. This can lead to a loud argument or one of you storming away.

- **The Benefit of Regulating your Emotions:** But when both of you learn how to regulate these feelings, you can stay rational and calm, making accurate assessments of what is happening and freeing yourself from the negative impact of another's feelings. You don't need to shout back when your partner shouts at you or catch their anxiety when they are fretting about bills. Remaining calm during these emotions will help steer your relationship to a better place, even in the face of difficulties or stress.

- **Practice Exercises for Relaxation Together:** Every day for the following eight weeks, start practicing exercises for relaxation with your loved one. You will find that this helps both of you manage your feelings instead of letting them drive you apart.

These tips, along with the key points in the last chapter, will help you guide your relationship to a better place. Building awareness in your relationship and working against catching emotions like fear, anxiety, or anger from each other is a great first step to take.

CHAPTER 6: HOW EMOTIONAL INTELLIGENCE HELPS YOU WITH CONFIDENCE

When we don't have enough emotional intelligence, our self-esteem suffers. We must pause in order to handle what is bothering us so we can learn to become joyful and at peace with ourselves and in life. One of the most important factors of EQ is confidence in yourself. This quality is nearly always there in the people that others respect and admire. People who feel positively toward themselves, free of arrogance, are the people who we consider to have their act figured out.

What does a Healthy Self-Confidence Look Like?

Having self-confidence means having a balanced and positive perspective about who you are and consists of the conviction that you can accomplish whatever you want. When problems pop up, a confident person will continue working to get through the issue, while someone who isn't as confident would probably not persist and may never begin the task to begin with. Getting through setbacks and feeling proud when we have achieved something is an important part of building up your confidence, even when the goals are small to begin with.

Insecurity is something that everyone in this world has struggled with before in their lives. But did you know that becoming more emotionally intelligence can help you build self-esteem? Insecurity comes on as the result of letting insecure, often irrational thoughts take over your mind and get to you. Since emotional intelligence is all about knowing how to manage your thoughts and feelings and still function successfully, this can be a great way to get your confidence growing and to have a healthy self-esteem. Let's look at some of the basics of this concept.

When you Know yourself, You're Comfortable with Who you are:

People who suffer from a lack of confidence often aren't sure who they are. They feel uncertain about their place in life, which makes them afraid to speak up. They constantly fear looking bad in front of others, which makes them act shy.

When you're Comfortable with Yourself, you aren't Insecure:

When you know yourself and are comfortable, you are not insecure around others. When you take the time to develop your emotional intelligence, your confidence will soar. So, how do you do this?

How to Improve your Confidence and EQ:

To begin improving your confidence, you can start by writing out a script of positivity for yourself. This will be a monologue that goes on inside of you to boost your sense of self-esteem. Think carefully about what this statement will say and write it down. Hold onto this and keep it somewhere that you can refer to it throughout the day. This will remind you of your journey to self-confidence. Here is an example of what the statement can look like:

"I respect myself and know that I am here for a reason. I care about being a kind person to others and try my best every day."

Your statement can be as long as you want, but a couple of sentences is a good start. If your statement doesn't perfectly align with who you are at the moment, you can spend your free time coming up with ways to make that a reality for you. If you are having trouble coming up with a mission statement, take some time to write about it and reflect. When you find that your life situation is very different from your statement, it can be difficult to feel truly self-confident.

Arrogance- a Symptom of Low Emotional Intelligence:

Having a low sense of self-confidence will negatively impact your life, but there is another problematic issue that usually comes along with a low EQ and that is arrogance. When someone acts overconfident, they are trying to make up for an inner lack, and this is a destructive quality to have. People who believe that they are better than others and act domineering are just as ineffective as people who have no confidence at all, because this trait leads to resentment and conflict.

When someone doesn't have confidence, they show a few key signs. These are trouble with admitting when they were wrong, the inability to say sorry, being pushy, or bragging to others. Although people who brag may appear confident at a first glance, when someone is truly confident, they don't feel this need because they already know of their worth and don't need to convince other people. When someone is overly concerned about appearing competent to others, they cannot admit when they are wrong, meaning that it's harder to take advice from well-meaning people around us. However, developing a strong EQ involves this step.

CHAPTER 7: HOW TO KNOW IF YOU'RE EMOTIONALLY INTELLIGENT

When you start working on raising your EQ, you will notice that you get stronger in certain aspects of your life. So, how can you tell if this quality is getting stronger in you? Here are some key signs that you are gaining emotional intelligence.

- **You Follow through on your Word:** Emotionally intelligent individuals do not bother claiming things that aren't true. Their word is important to them, and they always follow through on the promises they make to others around them.

- **Human Behavior Fascinates you:** People with a high EQ are intrigued by the behavior of humans. They pay attention to cues such as dialect, body language, and personality idiosyncrasies. Watching people help them discover what it is about others that makes them unique.

- **You are Okay with your Past:** The emotionally intelligent are able to move on from difficulties, facing life in the present moment. If you're too busy for regret and don't waste time ruminating on the past, it's a sign of a high EQ.

- **You Know your Faults and Strengths:** If you have a high EQ, you aren't afraid to admit your shortcomings since you know this is key to improving them. Instead of getting down about their faults, they use them as motivation to get even better and continually improve.

- **The Future doesn't Scare you:** Emotionally intelligent people never bother obsessing about events in the future that haven't occurred yet. They don't need to try to predict the details of every little event, because they enjoy life as it is. Instead of rushing through life to get to the next big thing, they are the active experiencers of their own lives.

- **When you're Upset, you Know Why:** With a high EQ, you don't let doubts and fears come in and take over your mind. You are an active explorer of your own environment and thoughts, finding reasons why your emotions are there and how you can use them.

- **You are Great at Listening:** If you're emotionally intelligent, you know how to listen. You don't just wait for your turn to talk, but actually relate to what the person speaking to you is saying, asking questions to show that you are engaged.

- **You are Fair at Work and your Personal Life:** You have a strong set of morals that you stick to, no matter what. Although values and morals differ from emotionally intelligent person to emotionally intelligent person, they all have high standards of excellence.

- **You Enjoy Helping Others:** If you enjoy helping people without needing a reason, it's a sign of a high EQ. You don't look at a situation where someone needs a hand and automatically wonder what's in it for you but get joy out of being able to help for the sake of helping itself.

- **You are Good at Reading Emotional Cues:** People with a high EQ are able to interpret nonverbal language, gestures, and facial expressions. They know how to look beyond words for the meaning in what someone is saying and how to interpret those signals effectively. This makes them great communicators.

- **Your Motivation comes from Within you:** If you know how to build lasting motivation, you probably have a high EQ. Instead of getting caught up on the end result and losing sight of the process, you know how to enjoy the entire journey, seeing each step as necessary and important. You never want to miss out on chances to learn, because they are happening all the time.

- **You can say "No":** If you have a hard time saying no to people, your emotional intelligence could need some work. It's impossible to please everyone and do everything at once, so setting time aside to prioritize your goals is important.

If you answered yes to any or all of these questions, congratulations! You're doing great at raising your EQ. Remember that you can always improve in this area, and that the journey is never over. If you still have a way to go, refer back to the tips in this book.

CONCLUSION

Thank you again for buying this book!

I hope this book was able to help you to understand what emotional intelligence truly means and help you find ways to develop yours to better relate to others and yourself. With this quality, there is no limit to what you can achieve in life and how you can affect others for the better.

The next step is to decide which ways you can improve your EQ and get to work doing it. Finally, if you enjoyed this book, then I'd like to ask you for a favor, would you be kind enough to leave a review for this book on Amazon? It'd be greatly appreciated!

Thank you and good luck!

Thank you!

Thank you for buying *Emotional Intelligence*. If you enjoyed reading this book, then I'd like to ask you for a favor, **would you be kind enough to leave a review for this book on Amazon? It'd be greatly appreciated!**

All my best wishes,

Josephine T. Lewis

www.ingramcontent.com/pod-product-compliance
Lightning Source LLC
Chambersburg PA
CBHW060217290526
45789CB00003B/1294